CECIL
RHODES

CECIL RHODES

THE MAN BEHIND THE STATUES

Kevin Shillington

BROWN
DOG
BOOKS

1st Edition (1992), published by the Rhodes Memorial Museum and Commonwealth Centre, Bishop's Stortford, now the Bishop's Stortford Museum and Rhodes Arts Complex

This revised edition published under licence by Brown Dog Books and The Self-Publishing Partnership Ltd, 10b Greenway Farm, Bath Rd, Wick, nr. Bath BS30 5RL

www.selfpublishingpartnership.co.uk

ISBN printed book: 978-1-83952-384-7
ISBN e-book: 978-1-83952-385-4

Cover design by Andrew Prescott
Internal design by Andrew Easton

Printed and bound in the UK
This book is printed on FSC certified paper

Photo acknowledgements: Unless otherwise stated after caption, all photos are reproduced by kind permission of the Bishop's Stortford Museum and Rhodes Arts Complex. The stamp on the back cover is from the collection of Michael New.

In memory of my late father,
who understood

Contents

PREFACE TO THE 2ND EDITION

Statues of historical figures are erected to celebrate their achievements and to keep alive their ideals. Following the death of Rhodes in 1902 and in the decade before the First World War, with Britain at the height of its imperial hegemony, an imperialist such as Cecil Rhodes was much in vogue and numerous statues were erected in his memory. A century on, they tell more about the beliefs and motives of those who commissioned and funded their erection than they do about the person portrayed or their impact upon history. While history is a constant process of revisiting and re-interpreting the past, what is surprising about the statues of Cecil Rhodes is that the reaction against them has been so long in coming.

On 9 March 2015, 21 years after the ending of *apartheid*, a student at the University of Cape Town (UCT) threw excrement at a statue of Cecil Rhodes that for generations had stood prominently on campus. The subsequent 'Rhodes Must Fall' movement, was unintentionally enflamed by the white Vice-Chancellor of UCT, Max Price, who defended Rhodes as a great man who should be honoured as such. The 'Rhodes Must Fall' movement, however, focussed more on the marginalisation of black students at UCT and the university's Eurocentric curricula than on the actual personality and deeds of Cecil Rhodes. There was a strong belief that it was not until the symbolic Rhodes statue was removed that serious attention could be paid to diversification in the University and to the decolonisation of education in South Africa as a whole. Within a month, the offending statue was removed.

The issue of statues of imperialists in Britain has been given focus by the country's widespread failure to recognise the reality of empire, upon which so much of the country's wealth and claim to 'world power' status was built. That reality was at the expense of the subjects of empire, their land and their resources. So much of British culture and attitude to the wider world is in silent denial of these realities.

In the Oxford of the Rhodes Scholars, high up on the front façade of Oriel College, overlooking the main street in the centre of Oxford, is a statue of Cecil Rhodes, a former benefactor of his old alma mater. It was erected in 1911 when the whole front

façade of Oriel College was rebuilt, with money from the Rhodes Estate. Following the success of the South African campaign, the 'Rhodes Must Fall Movement, Oxford' was formed to campaign for the removal of the Rhodes statue from its prominent position on the front of Oriel College. Oxford scholars and others of former colonial heritage objected that such a prestigious university of international renown, decades after the end of empire, should so proudly display a monument that clearly glorified a white supremacist and colonial conqueror. It was seen as a symbol of the lack of acceptance into British society of people of colour as truly English, even those for whom England was their place of birth.

Their campaign was roundly condemned from on high, most notably by Lord Chris Patten, the Chancellor of the University of Oxford and formerly the last colonial Governor of Hongkong (1992–97), who declared that if the protestors did not like Oxford as it was, they should go elsewhere. High-profile critics such as these accused Oxford's Rhodes Must Fall Movement of wanting to 'erase history'. But statues are not in themselves history. They are simply examples of people whom those in the present think most worthy of memorialising and celebrating.

At the time of writing, while the Rhodes statue remains in place, Oriel College has displayed a plaque acknowledging that Rhodes, 'a committed British colonialist, obtained his fortune through exploitation of minerals, land, and peoples of southern Africa. Some of his activities led to great loss of life and attracted criticism in his day and ever since.' The debate rages on.

For those who would partake in that debate I offer a brief account of the reality of Rhodes's life, his pursuit of wealth and power and what he did with that power in pursuing colonial conquest and in laying some of the foundations of South Africa's 20th century apartheid state.

Kevin Shillington,
October 2021.

CHAPTER 1

Birth and Early Life in England

Background

Cecil John Rhodes was born on 5 July 1853 in the Hertfordshire market town of Bishop's Stortford.

It was the sixteenth year of Queen Victoria's reign and Britain was a major world power. As the leading industrialised nation of Europe, Britain was destined within a few decades, and with the help of Cecil Rhodes, to reach the pinnacle of her imperial prowess. On the Continent, the Great Powers of Europe were gearing up for what was to become the Crimean War. At Westminster the Liberal peer Lord Aberdeen presided over a shaky coalition government and W.E. Gladstone had recently taken over the post of Chancellor of the Exchequer from his Tory rival Benjamin Disraeli. These two great parliamentarians of the mid-Victorian age were yet to assume the leadership of their respective parties.

Southern Africa, where Cecil Rhodes was to make his mark upon the world, was little known to most of the English population, though this was soon to change. Around the time of Cecil's birth, the missionary and explorer Dr David Livingstone was struggling through the swampy upper reaches of the Zambezi River on that first great trans-continental journey which was to make his a household name in England and which awakened British interest to the prospects of the interior of Africa.

The Rhodes family

Cecil was the sixth surviving child of the Reverend Francis William Rhodes, Vicar of Bishop's Stortford, and his second wife Louisa Peacock. The Rhodes family had for several generations been yeoman farmers, and brick- and tile-makers and traders in what is now the Islington district of north London. Reverend Francis Rhodes, educated at Harrow and Trinity College Cambridge, had been appointed Vicar of Bishop's Stortford in 1849. His wife, Louisa Peacock came from a Lincolnshire landed-gentry background. Her father was a country banker and Westminster MP at the time of Cecil's birth.

The Vicar had a modest private income from family land in Islington to supplement his meagre Church of England stipend so that, with careful housekeeping, the Rhodes family lived a moderately comfortable middle-class Victorian life. Mrs Rhodes employed ten servants to help her run the family home, her own time being taken up mostly in child-rearing: she gave birth to eleven children in sixteen years. The Rhodes family lived at first in the vicarage adjoining St Michael's Church in the centre of Bishop's Stortford, but in 1850 they moved to Netteswell House, a three-storeyed semi-detached Georgian house on the southern edge of town where Cecil was born. The vicarage, meanwhile, became part of the high school that had been founded by the Vicar and which he had put in the charge of his curate, Dr Goodman.

Goodman's High School, Bishop's Stortford where Cecil Rhodes and his brothers went to school, just across the lane from St Michael's Church

High School Bishops Stortford

The young Cecil

In 1862, at the age of nine, Cecil followed his three elder brothers to Goodman's High School, a mile's walk up the road from the family home. Cecil was thin and pale as a boy, somewhat untidy, and was reputed to have a 'girlish' way of talking. His boisterous elder brothers, Herbert and Frank, soon moved on to public school, but after that the family appears to have been pressed for funds for Cecil remained at Goodman's. This lack of preferment may have added to his competitive determination. His school interests were mostly history and the classics, and he left school at the age of fifteen with a classics prize and first-class honours in the Cambridge Local Examination.

Rhodes as a young schoolboy

Frank and Ernest were about to enter the army and the eldest son, Herbert, had just left home to 'seek his fortune' in South Africa. Cecil was undecided about his future. Reverend Rhodes hoped he would follow him in holy orders, but the young Cecil hoped for something more ambitious. Although for the next year and a half he studied under his father and helped him with St Michael's Sunday School, whenever possible he got away to stay with his maiden aunt Sophy Peacock, travelling on the new Northern and Eastern Railway line to the Manor House at Sleaford in Lincolnshire. Here he experienced and enjoyed the social and sporting life of a country squire. He confided to Aunt Sophy that he wanted to be a barrister rather than go into the Church, although he did not want to disappoint his father. In either case a university education was essential and without money this would not prove easy. His family, meanwhile, were not keen that he should study law and he was considered 'too delicate' for the army.

An invitation from South Africa

Towards the end of 1869 a letter arrived from Herbert inviting

Cecil to join him for a while in Natal, the small British colony on the south-eastern seaboard of South Africa. It seemed the obvious solution and the prospect of adventure excited the sixteen-year-old youth. It would give him a chance to grow up and prove himself and it postponed any firm decision about university and the long-term future. There is no firm evidence that he was sent to South Africa because his health was poor. This appears to have been an idea that developed later and was picked up by some of his earlier biographers.

Cecil sailed for South Africa aboard the ageing wooden sailing ship *Eudora* in June 1870, just two weeks short of his seventeenth birthday. Seventy-two days later the *Eudora* dropped anchor at the Natal port of Durban and Cecil Rhodes began the great imperial adventure that was to be his life in southern Africa.

CHAPTER 2

Southern Africa in 1870

The mineral revolution

The year 1870 is generally considered by historians to be a turning point in the history of South Africa. Even many of those alive in South Africa at the time were aware that the possibility of a new era was opening before them. 1870 marked the beginning of South Africa's mineral revolution upon which its present industrialisation was to be based. It began in the early 1870s with the discovery of the world's richest deposits of diamonds, and it continued in the 1880s with the discovery of the world's largest deposits of gold. The combination of the two was to transform the whole shape and tone of South African society. Up until that time South Africa had generally been regarded in England as a sleepy backwater of the British colonial empire - no more than an important staging post on the sea route to India, and even that was losing its significance with the opening of the Suez Canal in 1869.

The land and its people

Britain had seized control of the Cape during the Napoleonic Wars of the early nineteenth century. Before that it had been a colony of the Dutch East India Company since 1652. Until recent decades, most books on South Africa took a Eurocentric view of the region's history, tending to begin with this European colonisation, as though the indigenous African population had no prior history or claim to the region. In fact, as archaeologists have revealed over the past half-century, South Africa has a very ancient history of human habitation.

The region abounds in evidence of the activities of stone-age hunter-gatherers, stretching back for tens of thousands of years. And for at least 2,000 years they had been herding sheep and goats, and probably cattle as well. It was descendants of these hunting and herding people whom the first Dutch settlers met and traded with at the Cape in the seventeenth century.

The hunters and herdsmen were to be found mostly in the

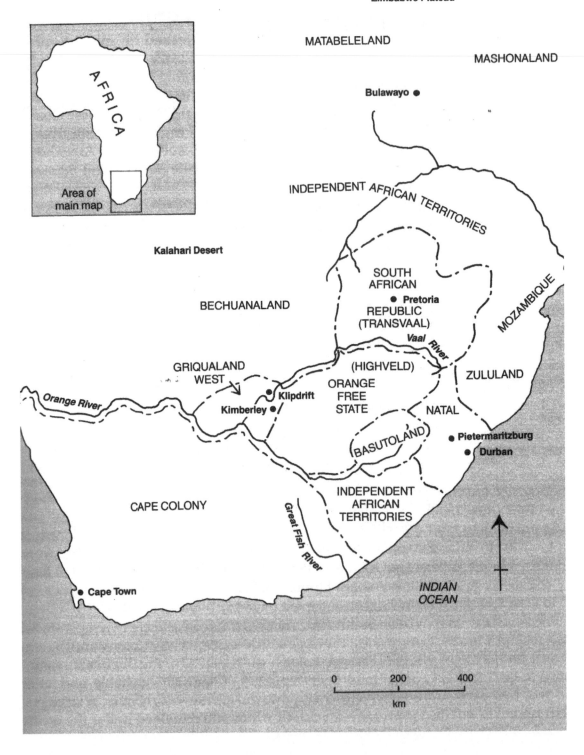

Zimbabwe Plateau

MATABELELAND

MASHONALAND

Bulawayo ●

INDEPENDENT AFRICAN TERRITORIES

Kalahari Desert

BECHUANALAND

SOUTH
AFRICAN
REPUBLIC
(TRANSVAAL)

● Pretoria

Vaal River

MOZAMBIQUE

GRIQUALAND
WEST

(HIGHVELD)

ORANGE
FREE
STATE

ZULULAND

Orange River

Klipdrift

Kimberley ●

NATAL

BASUTOLAND

● Pietermaritzburg
● Durban

CAPE COLONY

Great Fish River

INDEPENDENT
AFRICAN
TERRITORIES

● Cape Town

INDIAN
OCEAN

Area of
main map

AFRICA

0   200   400

km

drier, south-western part of southern Africa. In the better- watered south-eastern region and on the central highveld the indigenous African people practised a mixture of crop cultivation and closely controlled cattle-keeping. Self-sufficient African farmers, smelting and forging their own iron tools, had been living, working and trading in this region since at least the third or fourth century AD. Over the centuries these small-scale mixed farming communities had organised themselves into a number of powerful kingdoms, such as the Amaxhosa and Amazulu in the south-east, and the Basotho and Batswana on the highveld.

The expansion of white settlement

During the eighteenth and early nineteenth centuries the descendants of the original Dutch settlers (known as 'Boers', from the Dutch word for farmer) trekked further and further eastwards from the Cape in search of new hunting territory and grazing land for their large flocks of sheep and herds of cattle. On their way they fought an everlasting battle with the indigenous African hunters, herders and farmers who rightly saw the white man's approach as an invasion of their ancestral lands. By the late eighteenth century this eastwards expansion had been halted by the powerful Amaxhosa kingdoms east of the Great Fish River. In the 1830s a large number of eastern Cape Boers moved up onto the highveld in a movement which was later to be glorified by their descendants as the 'Great Trek', but which was in effect an invasion. After a series of dramatic conflicts with the Africans of the region, they established two Boer republics, the Orange Free State, north of the Orange River, and the Transvaal or South African Republic, north of the Vaal River. These were independent of British control from the Cape, although in the 1840s the British had in fact taken over the Boers' south-eastern coastal republic to create the British colony of Natal (see map on page 6).

    The South Africa of 1870 thus consisted of two separate British territories, the large south-western Cape Colony and the smaller south-eastern colony of Natal. On the highveld were two precarious Boer republics, financially unstable and in perpetual conflict with their African neighbours, while a large portion of present-day South Africa remained under the control of independent

Opposite page:
Southern Africa in 1871

African kingdoms that were powerful enough to resist any further white encroachment on their land. By the late 1860s any such encroachment would require large-scale military backing which only Britain could provide. However, the British Government was not prepared to invest in major military conflict in the interior – until, that is, the discovery of diamonds in 1870-71, just beyond the northern boundary of the Cape Colony.

The economy before 1870

The economy of southern Africa up till 1870, for black and white alike, was dominated by rural pursuits. Most communities were relatively self-sufficient, growing their own foodstuffs and trading with the surplus. The main exports were wool from the Cape Colony and ostrich feathers and ivory from the interior. The main imports were clothing and guns.

The small white settler community of Natal was experimenting with several different agricultural crops, such as sugarcane along the humid coastal region. Inland, some were trying cotton to take advantage of the soaring prices that could be obtained for cotton during the American Civil War of the early 1860s. Herbert Rhodes had been one of the first English settlers to try cotton planting in the Umkomaas Valley district, south of the colony's capital of Pietermaritzburg (see map on page 6) and so it was to a fledgling cotton farm that Cecil Rhodes first came in September 1870.

Rhodes's arrival at his brother's farm

Herbert Rhodes was not at home to welcome his younger brother to the Umkomaas Valley farm. He had been caught up in the 'diamond fever' that was taking a hold of so many white South Africans during those heady months of 1870. After planting his first crop of cotton in October 1869, the elder Rhodes had joined a party of English adventurers and proceeded to 'the diamond-fields' in the region of the lower Vaal, just west of the Orange Free State. There his party was instrumental in uncovering the first major 'river-diggings' site at Klipdrift (later renamed Barkly West) in March 1870. By May Herbert Rhodes was back in Natal in time for harvesting his first crop of cotton only to find it had suffered badly from disease and lost him money. He headed back to the more profitable diamond-fields and did not return until a month after Cecil's arrival.

Learning the business of farming

The seventeen-year-old Cecil does not seem to have been too non-plussed by the initial absence of his elder brother and he impressed his brother's acquaintances with his quiet self-confidence and evident maturity. Despite his youth and inexperience at working with his hands or supervising labourers, the serious-minded gangling youth adapted quickly to the new life and wrote home enthusiastic letters to his mother and to Aunt Sophy.

The farmhouse on the Rhodes farm was nothing more than an oblong mud-brick hut furnished simply with two beds and a table. But for the next six months, after Herbert's return, the two brothers lived there, supervising their Amazulu labourers in planting a new crop of cotton, improving the homestead and planning improvements to the farm. Cecil appears to have taken the financial side of the farming business more seriously than his elder brother who was more interested in the social life of Pietermaritzburg. Cecil was intent on maximising the farm's return, to save enough money to put himself through university at Oxford. Although naturally excited by Herbert's stories of the potential wealth of the diamond-fields, it sounded a precarious business to him and Cecil's financial instincts at this stage were on the side of caution.

By March 1871 Herbert could stand the boredom no longer and he set off again for the diamond-fields, leaving his younger brother to supervise the cotton harvest on his own. As Cecil Rhodes celebrated his eighteenth birthday in July 1871 with the successful completion of the cotton harvest, Herbert was busy staking out claims at the fabulously rich diamond 'mine' that had just been uncovered at Colesberg Kopje, a small hillock some ten to fifteen miles south of the diggings on the Vaal. Known at first as 'New Rush' and later renamed Kimberley mine (see map on page 6), after the British Secretary of State for the Colonies, Lord Kimberley, this was soon to prove to be the richest diamond mine the world had ever known.

Back in Natal, as he sold the proceeds of his first cotton harvest, the younger Rhodes realised that the cotton boom was over, and he would stand a better chance of making his fortune through joining his brother at the diamond-fields. Thus it was that at the beginning of October 1871 Rhodes abandoned plans to plant another crop of cotton and set off on the 400-mile trek, riding a pony ahead of his ox-drawn cart, the latter being tended by a handful of servants.

CHAPTER 3

Rhodes, Kimberley and Oxford

Rhodes at the diamond fields

By the time Rhodes arrived at the diamond-fields in November 1871, a ramshackle, dusty township of tents and corrugated-iron huts had sprung up around the principal diamond mine which itself was divided into thirty-foot square claims. Each of these was normally sub-divided into quarter shares and often eighths, so that Herbert was one of the better-off claimholders in that he owned a total of three complete claims. A number of Africans had staked out claims in the early years of the diamond-fields, but white colonists made strenuous efforts to exclude them, and in due course colonial authorities legally banned Africans from holding claims. Their role was to be that of labourer, thus although the white claim-holders called themselves 'diggers', it was black Africans who did the actual digging.

Dick Launder's Camp, Kimberley, 1872. Herbert Rhodes is holding the kettle, Frank Rhodes, in white shirt, is sitting at the table and Cecil is seated on extreme right

Cecil Rhodes has often been portrayed as having arrived at the diamond-fields as a penniless youth, with the clear implication that his subsequent huge wealth was entirely self-made. In fact, he arrived with a considerable nest-egg of £2000, which his Aunt Sophy had advanced to him before he left England. This was the equivalent today of at least a quarter of a million pounds – no small sum for a gangling youth of seventeen. In trusting Cecil with such a large sum, Aunt Sophy had made a wise investment for it was not long before her nephew was buying into claims of his own. Within a few weeks of Cecil's arrival, Herbert left the diamond-fields for home, once more leaving his inexperienced brother to run the business: an indication, not only of his own restless nature, but also of his trust in the maturity and business acumen of his younger brother, a trust which was to be rewarded beyond Herbert's wildest dreams.

British annexation of the diamond-fields

Around the time of Herbert's departure, the British Government formally annexed the diamond-fields, over-riding the territorial claims of both Boer republics as well as local African chiefs. The intention was to join it to the Cape Colony in due course, although this was not finally completed until 1880. In the meantime, the

The first horse whim was used at Kimberley mine in 1874. As the mine got deeper, they gradually replaced hand tackle in lowering and hoisting buckets. In the 1880s the horse whim was overtaken by steam power

territory became the British Crown Colony of Griqualand West. Its administrative capital was the township that had grown around the Colesberg Kopje mine which had by then been renamed Kimberley.

A partnership, illness and the first Will

In about February 1872 Rhodes joined in business partnership with Charles Dunell Rudd. It was a partnership which was to last, in one form or another, for the rest of his business career. Rudd was about ten years older than Rhodes (still then not yet nineteen) and he had a wide range of business interests. He was a merchant, dealing in ropes, shovels, buckets and the general paraphernalia of diamond digging. And he was an insurance broker and diamond buyer as well as a claimholder. Almost immediately the new partners began buying into the neighbouring mine of De Beers where claims were generally cheaper and easier to work.

Soon after the new partnership had been formed Rhodes suffered something like a mild heart-attack. It badly frightened him for he was still very young, and he began to develop a foreboding that he would suffer an early death. It was while recovering from this illness that he drew up the first of the many wills he was to write. In it he left all his wealth to the Secretary of State for the Colonies to be used for the extension of the British Empire. In sentiment it was typical of that of many colonial Englishmen of the time, although Rhodes's was unusual in that wills like this usually left their money to the Queen. It might have been passed off as no more than a fit of youthful patriotism, but for the fact that in the case of Cecil Rhodes it was the germ of an idea which was to remain with him for the rest of his life and be developed into the 'great idea' that was to dominate his lifelong dreams of empire.

Back to England

In August 1873 Rhodes returned to England a reasonably wealthy man. His mother was ill at home, and it was time he signed up for Oxford, for which he now had the money. He entered Oriel College that October although he was still unsure about his long-term future. He appears to have had a great desire for self-esteem among his fellow men and at this stage was still considering a career as a barrister. To this end he began attending dinners at the Inner Temple to keep open the option of qualifying for the Bar.

In November 1873, in the middle of his first term at Oxford, his mother died, and Rhodes was devastated. He had had a close relationship with his mother, and it may have been her death that led to his decision to go back to Africa. Leaving Oxford after only one term, he returned to Kimberley in January 1874 and threw himself energetically into the business of making money.

Business thrives

In Rhodes's absence Rudd had looked after his business interests in Kimberley. During 1873 the partners had invested in an ice-making machine for cooling people's drinks in the stifling summer months. On Rhodes's return in 1874 he and Rudd won the contract for pumping out the floodwater that was causing havoc in the deepening mine of Kimberley. Showing a newfound daring and willingness to gamble, Rhodes had won the bid for the pumping contract before he even owned a pump. While he waited for machinery to be carted by ox-wagon from 600 miles away at the Cape, he scoured the countryside until he found a pump belonging to a Boer eight days' journey away in the Orange Free

De Beers Mine in 1872

State. After several days of camping on the poor man's doorstep, the budding young magnate persuaded the farmer to part with his steam-driven pump for £1000, a huge sum in those days.

There were four diamond mines within the bounds of the Kimberley township and Rhodes and Rudd regularly ploughed back all the funds that they could spare into buying up shares in the claims of the two largest mines, Kimberley and De Beers. The two men understood that in due course, as the mines reached deeper and deeper levels, large-scale amalgamation of claims was the only practical way to profit from diamonds in the long term.

Despite his steadily increasing wealth, Rhodes lived a spartan existence, sharing a sparsely furnished corrugated shack with various other bachelors. Never having any romantic interest in women, Rhodes preferred the company of men and declared that marriage only interfered with work. Although considerably younger than most of his friends and business colleagues, the tall, slim, shabbily dressed figure of Rhodes was inevitably a leader in their company and was respected for a business maturity well beyond his years. Even his closest associates always addressed him as 'Rhodes', never 'Cecil'.

An undergraduate at Oxford

In April 1876 Rhodes returned to England to renew his studies at Oxford. In what was to be his longest period away from Africa, he remained at Oxford until June 1878, completing all but one term of the required three-year residence at the university, only returning to Kimberley for a brief few months in the summer vacation of 1877. He did not make his mark in academic study at Oxford and was reputed to have carried around handfuls of diamonds in his pockets which he would produce and scatter on his desk during lectures that he thought were boring. With his experience of the world, the young man from Kimberley was unlikely to have fitted in with the general run of undergraduates of his day. Rhodes enjoyed the pursuits of a gentleman of means: he rode to the Drag Hounds, played polo and belonged to several exclusive clubs, including Vincent's and the Bullingdon. His social life appears to have centred around small private bachelor dinners at which he led debates on imperial themes. In these discussions he drew much

of his inspiration from the second century Roman philosopher/ emperor Marcus Aurelius whose book of *Meditations* was Rhodes's constant companion.

The 'Confession of Faith'

During this time at Oxford Rhodes was honing his 'great idea' and in June 1877, on the day he had been inducted into the fraternity of Freemasonry, he wrote a 'Confession of Faith'. The 'Confession' was a distillation of all the imperialist dreams of his boyhood years. It was the ultimate development of the theme of his first will. Reading it today, the audacity of it seems incredible and for this reason some historians have written it off as 'immature rubbish'. But for Rhodes it was deadly serious: he meant every word. It was a long rambling document, and a few brief phrases will give the gist of his beliefs:

'... We [the English] are the finest race in the world and ... the more of the world we inhabit the better it is for the human race. ... If we had retained America there would ... be millions more of English living. ... [Since] Africa is still lying ready for us it is our duty to take it. ... Why should we not form a secret society with but one object, the furtherance of the British Empire and the bringing of the whole civilized world under British rule.'

Rhodes had been quickly disillusioned with Freemasons, believing they wasted their potential as a secret band of brothers by focussing on 'the most ridiculous and absurd rites without an object and without an end'. He preferred to liken his secret society to that of the Jesuits whose efficiency, dedication and celibate sense of brotherhood he so admired. Those whom he expected to join his society would ideally be younger sons of the English middle classes like himself whose sole wish was to serve their country. In the 'Confession' and in the second will which he wrote in September 1877, following another heart-attack, Rhodes left all his wealth to the founding of this secret society for the infinite furtherance of the British Empire, and he nominated his friend Sidney Shippard, Attorney-General of Griqualand West, and the Colonial Secretary, Lord Carnarvon, as his trustees to see that his wishes would be carried out.

The 'Confession' of course was only an ultimate dream to which his future direction should be pointed. It was his 'great idea'. In the meantime, in his everyday life Rhodes remained an immensely practical man and was usually very cautious in his business dealings. The 'Confession' was written at a time of immense British imperial pride. Disraeli was Prime Minister and was expanding British influence everywhere. It was Disraeli who bought the Suez Canal for Britain and elevated Queen Victoria to be Empress of India in 1877. But despite the increasing jingoism of the period, it says much for Rhodes's charisma and skills of persuasion that he was able to sweep along so many hard-headed businessmen, politicians and colonial governors with his fantastic dreams.

In February 1878 Rhodes's father died and thereafter Rhodes the undergraduate appeared to lose interest in Oxford and the Inner Temple. Perhaps all along he had been trying to prove something to his father, who was always rather distant from his many sons. Whatever his exact motivation at this time, Rhodes left England for South Africa in June 1878 and only returned to Oxford to do his final term and take his pass degree in 1881.

CHAPTER 4

Southern Africa, Rhodes and Political Power, 1880-85

Changes in southern Africa

The southern Africa to which Rhodes returned in 1878 was a very different place from that which he had first seen only eight years previously. The mineral revolution that had started in Kimberley in the early 1870s, and in which Rhodes had played his part, had awoken southern Africa from its isolated rural slumber and wrought a profound change upon the region's social, economic and political life. Sizeable fortunes being daily won (and lost) in Kimberley by white colonists from as far afield as Cornwall, California and Australia, while local Africans who had been key players in the early discovery of diamonds, were legally excluded from holding claims in the developing diamond mines and were largely confined to the role of labourer. The effects of the sudden emergence in the far interior of a thriving modern city of between 20,000 and 30,000 people, however, were felt by black and white alike throughout the length and breadth of the sub-continent.

All eyes turned to Kimberley, not only for the fortune of its diamonds, but also as a market for its teeming population. The farmers of the highveld, both black and white, suddenly had a profitable cash market for their corn, for their cattle, and for firewood. But perhaps most significant of all, Kimberley acted like a human magnet, drawing in African migrant labour from as far away as Basutoland, Natal, the northern Transvaal and southern Mozambique. In Kimberley they could earn cash wages which, although only £1 a week, were nevertheless far higher than anywhere else in southern Africa and within a month was enough to buy a good muzzle-loading gun. As a result of these developments the period 1877 to 1885 was one of increasingly violent confrontation as those Africans already under white rule rose in rebellion and those still independent strongly resisted further attempts at white conquest.

Rhodes seeks political power

Just as South Africa had changed, so of course had Cecil Rhodes. Through his partnership with Rudd and others he was becoming one of the wealthier men in Kimberley, though by no means yet the wealthiest. His combination of business experience at Kimberley and academic years at Oxford had added a certain maturity to the youth of former years and in his 'Confession of Faith' he had articulated a goal for his life's work. Rhodes returned to Kimberley in 1878 with renewed vigour and sense of purpose and threw his boundless energy into combining increasing wealth at the diamond-fields with political power at the Cape.

Control of Griqualand West was transferred to the Cape Colony in November 1880 and Rhodes stood for election to the Cape Legislative Assembly. Only white men were allowed to stand for parliament and in what was virtually an all-white electorate, Rhodes shrewdly did not stand for Kimberley itself, where business rivalry might have marred his chances of election. He chose instead the nearby rural constituency of Barkly West. He had always seen himself as a country gentleman at heart and campaigning in the rural constituency of Barkly West opened his eyes to the interests of the Dutch-speaking farmers of the region. This was to prove an invaluable advantage in his later development of parliamentary alliances.

Rhodes entered the Assembly in 1881 and quickly made his mark in Cape politics. He eschewed the formal dress of parliament and insisted on wearing the casual flannels and loose jacket by which he was so well-known in Kimberley. He was no great orator, seldom preparing speeches, preferring to speak 'from the heart'. As a result, to the modern reader his speeches appear somewhat rambling and disjointed, for he threw out ideas as they occurred to him, often without having thought them through beforehand. Nevertheless, despite the high falsetto which his voice sometimes reached when he was excited, he always impressed the House with his forceful manner and the audacious way he spoke his mind.

Rhodes chaired several Select Committees and Commissions in the early 1880s, but his main concern at this time was to secure control of the northern hinterland of Kimberley from which came the labour for his mines and the industrial firewood for the steam engines now needed to power his winches, crushing gear and pumps.

Bechuanaland

To the north of Griqualand West lay a narrow strip of fertile land between the western border of the Transvaal and the dry expanse of the Kalahari Desert. It was the land of the Batswana and was known to the English as 'Bechuanaland'. This vital corridor of land was the 'road to the north' for British missionaries and traders from the Cape and the 'road to the diamond-fields' for potential African labourers from the interior. In this crucial zone, well-watered by a number of seasonal streams, lived several rival Batswana chiefdoms, already competing among themselves for the region's scarce resources. Proximity to Kimberley's insatiable market for food and firewood merely increased the value of the land and added urgency to the competition. At the same time, the eyes of the Transvaal Boers turned with envy upon the herds of Batswana cattle and the fertile land just beyond their western boundary. Towards the end of 1881 bands of Boer mercenaries joined the rival chiefdoms of Bechuanaland, stimulating local rivalries into open warfare.

As Transvaal Boers and other white mercenaries from Kimberley took over the running of the Bechuanaland wars, Rhodes viewed the turmoil with increasing anxiety. The Transvaal had recently won its freedom (in the first Anglo-Boer War of 1880-81) from a brief four-year period of British annexation. A new-found sense of Boer nationalism was in the air and anti-British feeling was running high in the Transvaal.

Rhodes cared nothing for the land rights of the local Batswana population, the sooner they were landless labourers, the more cheap labour there would be for the mines and other colonial enterprises. His prime concern was to prevent Bechuanaland from falling into the hands of the Transvaal for this would give the restored Boer Republic control over the southward flow of labour to the diamond-fields. At the same time, it would cut off ultimate British access to the potential wealth of the Central African interior.

In 1883 Rhodes's worst fears seemed confirmed when victorious Transvaal mercenaries declared two Boer 'republics', 'Stellaland' and 'Goshen', right across the Bechuanaland corridor to and from the north.

As Rhodes urged the Cape Government to accept Batswana

pleas for help and annex the region to the Cape, the Kuruman missionary John Mackenzie, with different priorities in mind, was rousing the humanitarian lobby in England on behalf of the Batswana cause and urging a preoccupied British Government to over-rule the mercenaries' action and extend imperial 'protection' to Bechuanaland. In February 1884 the British Government finally responded by extending informal 'protection' to the region and sending John Mackenzie himself as Deputy Commissioner to restore peace to Bechuanaland. In complete contrast to Rhodes, Mackenzie saw Britain as a 'protecting' imperial power, there to protect the land and civil rights of those Africans brought under British over-rule. He believed his role in Bechuanaland was to restore the Batswana to the lands they had lost to the mercenaries of Stellaland and Goshen. But with no military backing of his own he was unable to persuade or cajole a bunch of battle-hardened white mercenaries to voluntarily give up their land claims. From Cape Town Rhodes engineered the recall of Mackenzie and had himself appointed Deputy Commissioner in his place.

Bechuanaland becomes a British 'protectorate'

Rhodes had no compunction about sacrificing African land rights for the greater end of British imperial and local colonial interests. He quickly made a deal with the Stellaland mercenaries, promising to recognise all their claims to land on condition they agreed to annexation by the Cape. But he failed to achieve the same deal in neighbouring Goshen where determined Batswana resistance was preventing the white mercenaries from taking possession of the land. With the Transvaal Government daily threatening to annex both 'republics', Rhodes appealed for British military assistance. The British Government faced the strategic embarrassment of recent German annexation of South-West Africa (future Namibia - see map on page 30) and the prospect of a possible German-Transvaal power bloc across the 'road to the north'. They agreed to Rhodes's request and despatched a full- scale military expedition to Bechuanaland.

In the event it was an expedition which did not fire a single shot. The steady northward advance of 4,000 British troops under the command of Major-General Sir Charles Warren was enough

Military expedition in Bechuanaland: (front centre with hat in hand) Sir Gordon Sprigg, former Prime Minister of the Cape Colony (1878–81); (rear, left to right) C.J. Rhodes, Deputy Commissioner for Bechuanaland, 1884; Colonel F. Carrington, Commander of the Bechuanaland Border Police from 1885; Reverend John Mackenzie, Kuruman missionary and former Deputy Commissioner for Bechuanaland, 1884; and Major-General Sir Charles Warren, Commander of the Bechuanaland Expedition, 1884–85

to persuade the recalcitrant men of Goshen to retire into the Transvaal, only to re-emerge as willing transport drivers for the British expedition. Warren tactfully employed both former Deputy Commissioners, Mackenzie and Rhodes, as special advisers, thus enabling Rhodes to be present in January 1885 at a meeting on the banks of the Vaal between General Warren and the President of the Transvaal Republic, Paul Kruger. It was the first face to face meeting of these two rival giants of South African affairs.

The expedition is notable for the opportunity it afforded Warren of extending the British Protectorate into northern Bechuanaland, the territory of present-day Botswana. In terms of Rhodes's career, the Bechuanaland affair is important because, in the first place, it brought the name of 'Rhodes' to the attention of the British governing establishment. Secondly, it gave Rhodes himself the opportunity to visit Bechuanaland and talk with British military officers and elephant hunters who had first-hand experience of the far interior of southern Africa. The opportunity enabled him to develop a romantic and somewhat colourful view of the potential wealth of the land to the north of the Limpopo and Zambezi Rivers. It was during this time, in the early months of 1885, when the future of Bechuanaland was secure, that ideas of further British northward expansion began to take root in the fertile imagination of Cecil Rhodes.

In November 1885, during a visit to London, Rhodes wrote a series of letters to *The Times* in which he outlined his own role in the British acquisition of Bechuanaland. Carefully drafted with the aid of a close friend, the letters were a reply to criticism of him by General Warren. Rhodes's version of events exaggerated his own role out of all proportion to his actual contribution, but it helped convince British public opinion, and his earlier biographers, that the acquisition of Bechuanaland had been long planned by Rhodes as part of a far-reaching, grand imperial design for British expansion to the north as far as Egypt. A careful examination of the evidence reveals that Rhodes's initial interest in Bechuanaland was prompted by his own local mining interests in Kimberley. The 'inevitable' northward advance of white supremacy in southern Africa had been taken for granted in the minds of British imperialists since at least the 1850s. Rhodes was not unique in holding these views and it was only from 1885 that he began to elaborate specific schemes for further, specifically British, northward expansion.

CHAPTER 5

Rhodes, the De Beers Monopoly and Gold

Although Rhodes was extensively occupied in his new political duties in Cape Town and in Bechuanaland, his main energies in the 1880s were directed towards acquiring wealth and power in Kimberley.

The De Beers Mining Company

In April 1880 Rhodes and a group of partners formed the De Beers Mining Company with initial capital of £200,000. Rhodes, who started as Company Secretary, had by 1883 become its President. With his imaginative flair and dogged determination, there is little doubt that he controlled the direction and policy of the company so that, although he was not personally the largest shareholder, it was considered by all outside the boardroom to be Rhodes's company. The purpose of the new company was to buy out all the other companies in De Beers mine, an aim which they had achieved by 1887. By then the company's capital had risen to well over £2 million. Rhodes's personal annual income has been estimated at around £50,000 in 1885. This was at a time when anyone earning as much as £1,000 a year was very comfortably off. Rhodes was clearly an extremely wealthy man.

Rhodes had been one of the first to realise in the 1870s that the most efficient and most profitable way to mine and market diamonds would be to amalgamate all the claims under a single company – in effect to create a monopoly. He knew that gem diamonds were expensive for two basic reasons, their beauty and their rarity. The former was constant, but the latter was not. Since the discovery of the Kimberley mines, diamonds were no longer rare, and this fact alone had caused a drastic drop in diamond prices in the early 1870s. Rhodes argued that the only way to recreate that rarity was to control and restrict the production and marketing of diamonds and this could only be done by ending competition between rival companies. At the same time, Rhodes's

De Beers Company was able to demonstrate that the economies of scale brought in by amalgamation would further enhance profits by immediately reducing costs of production.

In 1887, with the whole of De Beers mine now firmly under his control, Rhodes began the assault on the companies of the larger and richer mine of Kimberley itself. Here the main rival was the Central Mining Company, controlled by a former music-hall artist from the East End of London called Barnett Isaacs, popularly known as Barney Barnato. Barnato had arrived in Kimberley in 1873 with a case full of cigars and an ambition to equal that of Cecil Rhodes. By 1887 Barnato controlled half of Kimberley mine and had accumulated more capital in the Central Company than there was in the whole of the De Beers mine.

Although Barnato was often scorned by Rhodes's business colleagues for his humble origins, in the contest which followed Rhodes himself hardly displayed the kind of business principles considered befitting a gentleman. The final battle for control of the diamond-fields brought out a ruthless streak in Rhodes that

The Board of De Beers Consolidated Mining Company, 1893: (left to right, standing) E. Bernheim, W.H. Craven (Secretary), Gardner F. Williams (General Manager), L. Breitmeyer, Lieutenant Colonel Harris; (sitting) Woolf Joel, C.E. Nind, H. Mosenthal, C.J. Rhodes (Life Member), B.J. Barnato (Life Member), Francis Oats and G.W. Compton

made some of his more genteel companions blanch. When the stakes were as high as this, Rhodes showed himself to be totally without scruple. Over the next twelve months he manipulated the stock exchange in a manner that would put him in gaol today. He drove share-prices alternately up and down, deliberately bankrupting companies and assiduously accumulating shares in all the remaining independent companies in the Kimberley mine. By early 1888 there was only De Beers and Barnato's Central Company left.

Amalgamation and Monopoly

In his final assault Rhodes had the backing of the European financier Lord Rothschild from whom he borrowed £1 million. For two months colonial life in Kimberley virtually ground to a halt as all eyes turned upon the battle of the giants. Barnato was no fool. He appreciated the advantages of amalgamation just as much as Rhodes; it was simply a matter of which of them would control it. Through meeting after meeting the stronger personality of Rhodes steadily wore down the financially more powerful Barnato until a deal was finally struck.

The cheque for £5,338,650 paid by De Beers Consolidated Mining Company to the liquidators of the Kimberley Central Diamond Mining Company for the Kimberley mine, 18 July 1889

In March 1888 the two companies amalgamated into a new De Beers Consolidated Mining Company which then bought out the remaining companies in the two smaller mines of Bultfontein and Dutoitspan. By 1889 Rhodes's new company had a complete monopoly of all diamond mining in Kimberley. With the power of monopoly, the company was able to lay off hundreds of workers. The remaining African mine labourers were confined to fenced compounds, their wages lowered, and all aspects of their lives strictly controlled. With monopoly control Rhodes was able to reduce the number of diamonds coming onto the market, and the price of diamonds duly rose. Within a year the cost of production was as little as a third of the world market price.

Gold on the Witwatersrand

Before Rhodes reached the final stages of sewing up his diamond empire in Kimberley, however, the centre of financial attention shifted to the Transvaal. In 1886 prospectors had uncovered an outcrop of gold-bearing rock along a ridge of barren land 30 miles south of Pretoria (see map on page 30). It was to prove to be the richest deposit of gold the world had ever seen. In the centre of this ridge, the Witwatersrand ('white water's ridge'), there sprang up within a few short years the largest African city south of Cairo and it was named Johannesburg.

Most of Kimberley's powerful mining capitalists rushed to 'the Rand', as it was called, to stake out and buy up gold mining claims. Rhodes surprised his business rivals by his initial caution over gold, but gold was unfamiliar to him and when he had been at the Witwatersrand for less than a month, news arrived from Kimberley that his young friend Neville Pickering, with whom he had shared his tiny house in Kimberley for four years, was dying. Rhodes returned to Kimberley immediately, just in time to be at Pickering's deathbed. He was devastated by the death of his closest friend and distracted from the Rand at a critical moment in its early development. When he finally got round to buying gold claims in any large quantity, most of the best ones had already been snapped up and he had to pay over the odds for those he did acquire. Nevertheless, he bought enough to found a company called Consolidated Goldfields of South Africa which by 1890 was one of the three largest gold mining companies on the Rand.

As he fought his final battle with Barnato, Rhodes was already evolving other plans that would more than make up for his initial disappointment on the Rand. It had long been suspected that ancient African gold-workings on the Zimbabwe Plateau (see map on page 30) might provide the clue to huge underground deposits of gold-bearing rock north of the Transvaal. Rhodes devised a bold plan whereby he would outstrip his rivals by capturing control of his own exclusive 'second Rand' north of the Limpopo and thus at the same time further his long-term grand design of British imperial expansion.

CHAPTER 6

Rhodes and the Founding of 'Rhodesia'

The Amandebele Kingdom

The principal African power on the Zimbabwe Plateau was the Amandebele (Matabele) Kingdom ruled by Lobengula. The Amandebele were cattle-keepers and maize farmers who had originated as an offshoot of the Amazulu Kingdom in the 1820s and had settled on the Zimbabwe Plateau in about 1840. They brought with them a highly disciplined military organisation that enabled them to dominate the region. Their army consisted of a series of age regiments, based upon those who were initiated into manhood in the same year. The regiments lived in military villages positioned at strategic points around the Kingdom. From there, they were able to protect the security of the Kingdom from outside attack and at the same time conduct punitive raids against their neighbours. From his capital of Bulawayo (see map), Lobengula exercised loose control over some of the Mashona chiefdoms to his east, expecting them to pay an annual tribute of food or hunting produce.

A fraudulent concession

Following the discovery of gold on the Rand in 1886 Bulawayo was inundated with white speculators and prospectors all seeking Lobengula's permission to prospect in his country. Rhodes feared that 'Matabeleland' would 'fall' to the Germans or to the Transvaal before he himself was ready to act, and he persuaded his friend Sidney Shippard, by then Administrator of Bechuanaland, to send the former missionary John Moffat to Lobengula to forestall his rivals. Moffat had formerly worked among the Amandebele, he spoke Isindebele and was able to earn Lobengula's trust. They concluded a treaty in February 1888 by which Lobengula undertook not to make a deal with any other power without first consulting Britain. The following month, Rhodes founded his new

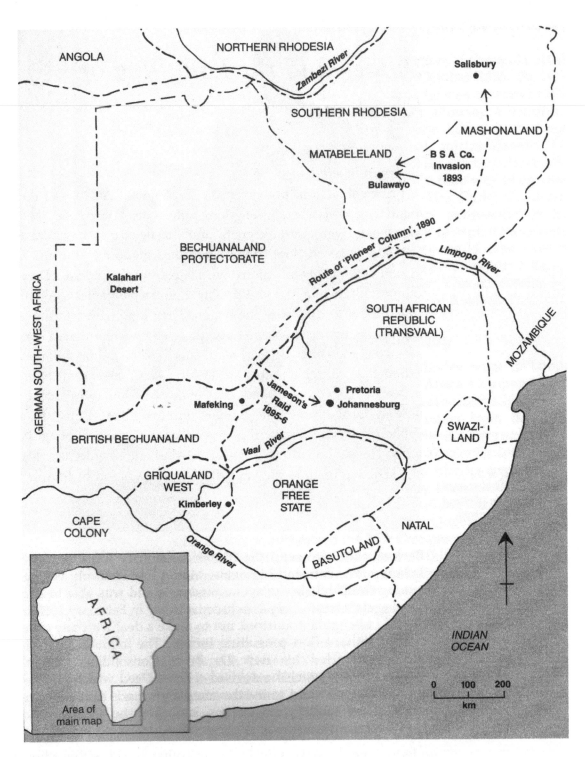

Southern Africa in
the 1890s

De Beers Consolidated Mining Company, for which he devised a Trust Deed that allowed him, as life governor, to use the company's funds to acquire any asset of any kind by any means, including the acquisition of territory in Central Africa. All he needed now was some form of concessionary authority from Lobengula to satisfy British Government approval. To this end he despatched to Bulawayo a three-man team, headed by his long-time partner Charles Rudd.

After two months of hard negotiation, Lobengula finally signed the 'Rudd Concession' on 30 October 1888. So far as Lobengula understood the concession, he was to receive £100 a month and 1000 rifles in exchange for allowing a handful of white men to dig for gold in his country. In fact, he had been duped. The Concession was deliberately mistranslated to him by the resident missionary, Reverend Helm, who believed that removal of the pagan Lobengula was the only way to persuade the Amandebele to turn to Christianity. The Rudd Concession gave Rhodes and his agents permission to take 'whatever action they consider necessary' to exploit the minerals of the Kingdom. In other words, they could take over the Kingdom itself if they considered it was 'necessary'! Back in Kimberley Rhodes crowed triumphantly: 'Our concession is so gigantic it is like giving a man the whole of Australia!'

Top Right: Umshete, Below Right:: Babyjane, Lobengula's delegates to the British Government to protest the fraudulent concession. Photo, Zimbabwe National Archives

The British South Africa Company

Armed with the Rudd Concession, Rhodes went to London where he founded the British South Africa (BSA) Company, using funds from

De Beers. With the backing of the Rothschilds he was soon able to attract enthusiastic investors from the British establishment. Rhodes charmed his way through British ruling circles and even won himself an invitation from the Queen to visit her at Windsor Castle.

Members of the 'Pioneer Column' at Mafeking on the eve of the Column's departure. Seated, l. to r. Dr Leander Starr Jameson and Dr Rutherford Harris were among Rhodes's closest confidants. Frederick Courtney Selous, an ivory hunter with long experience of Matabeleland, was official scout to the expedition, while A.R. Colquhoun was to become the BSA Company's Administrator in Mashonaland until 1891 when he was succeeded by Jameson

In October 1889 he was granted a Royal Charter which authorised the BSA Company to run the territory north of the Limpopo under the authority of the British flag, to set up all the paraphernalia of government and to profit from any surplus of revenue. Furthermore, Rhodes so impressed the principal members of the Board that they gave him the power of attorney to act as he saw fit, without their prior consultation. Thus, Rhodes had complete control.

Although Lobengula by this time realised what he had signed and had rejected the original concession, the British Government ignored Amandebele protests. Rhodes saw that Lobengula was the only real barrier standing between him and his future colony and he devised a secret plan to kidnap or assassinate the King. But the two amateur secret agents sent north to do the deed got drunk while travelling through Bechuanaland and talked openly about their mission.

Above: The 'Pioneer Column' form a laager on the banks of the Tuli River in June 1890 prior to building a fort on the south bank

Right: Soldiers of the Amandebele army near the Tuli River, June 1890, investigating the encroaching the BSA Company's hostile-looking 'Pioneer Column' passing by on the borders of their kingdom. Photo, Zimbabwe National Archives

Word got back to the British High Commissioner and the scheme was hastily cancelled and hushed up. Rhodes decided on an alternative scheme whereby he would circumvent Lobengula and establish his initial colony to the east of the Kingdom in Mashonaland. To this end he recruited 200 white settlers with promises of free land and fifteen gold claims each. They were to be accompanied by a further

200 mounted police, heavily armed with rifles and several Maxim guns, the latest weapon of destruction, a machine-gun mounted on wheels. This colonising 'Pioneer' column made its way across the Tuli River just north of the Limpopo and carefully skirted round the southern and eastern edge of the Amandebele Kingdom. When they reached the heart of Mashonaland, in September 1890, they established a township near the African village of Harare. They named their new colonial capital 'Salisbury', after the British Prime Minister of the day. It was to be renamed Harare following the independence of Zimbabwe 90 years later.

The invasion of Matabeleland

The 'pioneers' quickly spread out to stake their claims to farms, although their main concern was to investigate the country's old, abandoned gold-workings. They soon discovered, however, that the ancient Mashona miners had been more thorough than they had supposed and there were no easy fortunes to be made in Mashonaland.

With the BSA Company's investors expecting an early dividend, Rhodes had to find some financial reward from somewhere and he turned his attention once more to his original goal, the Amandebele Kingdom. The Kingdom's huge herds of cattle, fertile land and possible mineral wealth were tempting for the disappointed colonists, and they were eager for the fray. After a minor border dispute between Lobengula and the Company, and with the tacit approval of the British High Commissioner in Cape Town, Rhodes authorised an invasion of Matabeleland.

Lobengula is reputed to have commented:

> Did you ever see a chameleon catch a fly? The chameleon gets behind the fly and remains motionless for some time, then he advances very slowly and gently, first putting forward one leg and then another. At last, when well within reach, he darts out his tongue and the fly disappears. England is the chameleon, and I am that fly.

The invasion began in November 1893 with a flying-column of horsemen and Maxim guns. It was led by Rhodes's long-term friend and admirer Dr Leander Starr Jameson. Although greatly outnumbered by the Amandebele army, Jameson's tiny force used its superior weaponry to cut its way through Amandebele ambushes and reach Bulawayo in December. Lobengula had fled, leaving his capital in flames. The ageing King is believed to have died during flight and the victorious Jameson declared that as the BSA Company had assumed the authority of the dead Lobengula, all Amandebele land and cattle now belonged to the Company. In practise the Amandebele King had never personally owned all the land and cattle of the Kingdom; but in the months that followed, cattle and farms were given out piecemeal to the jubilant white victors and the value of BSA Company shares rose on the London Stock Exchange.

Northern Rhodesia

Meanwhile, in 1889 Britain had proclaimed the Central African Protectorate over what was to become Nyasaland (modern Malawi). This was left under BSA Company administration (until 1907), and Rhodes had paid his friend Sir Harry Johnston, Administrator of the Protectorate, a subsidy of £10,000 to help him militarily crush those Africans who showed any reluctance to accept British overrule. In return for this favour, in the early 1890s Johnston arranged for Rhodes's agents to penetrate the territory west of Nyasaland, fraudulently cajoling chiefs into signing treaties that effectively gave their country to the BSA Company. Where resistance was offered, Johnston supplied troops, and the maxim gun prevailed. With Rhodes's agents having already bluffed their way into possession of the mineral rights of Barotseland, in the west of the territory, by 1895 the whole of the country north of the Zambezi had become a further 'protectorate' for the BSA Company, soon to be known as 'Northern Rhodesia' (modern Zambia). The BSA Company was to use the Barotseland agreement to claim the 'mineral rights' to the whole of Northern Rhodesia, including the fabulously rich 'Copperbelt', which was in fact outside Barotseland. This raked in an enormous fortune for the Company, right up to the eve of Zambian independence in 1964.

Thanks to Rhodes' combination of fraudulent treaty-making and military force, British authority now stretched as far as the southern shores of Lake Tanganyika. Further expansion northwards was blocked by the Belgians in the Congo and the Germans in

Rhodes's lieutenants, assembled in Kimberley for a final briefing, May 1890, just before the departure of the 'Pioneer Column': (sitting, l. to r.) James Rochford Maguire, one of the three men whom Rhodes had sent to negotiate the Rudd Concession with Lobengula in 1888; Sir Harry Johnston, Rhodes's paid agent while British Commissioner and Consul-General north of the Zambezi; Rhodes; A. R. Colquhoun, the BSA Company's first Administrator of Mashonaland; (standing l. to r.) James Grant, explorer, one of Rhodes's treaty-making agents north of the Zambezi, 1890–91; John Moir, Nyasaland trader and one of Rhodes's active agents in the region; and Joseph Thomson, experienced explorer who, like Grant, was about to become one of Rhodes's treaty-making agents north of the Zambezi, 1890–91

Tanganyika (today's Tanzania). Rhodes's attempts to establish a 'Cape to Cairo' telegraph line and railway were similarly thwarted by imperial politics and costs. The railway line did not cross the Zambezi until a year after Rhodes's death and even then, it only went as far as the Northern Rhodesian Copperbelt. Ironically, it was to be Communist Chinese capital and labour which finally extended the railway line to Dar-es-Salaam in Tanzania in 1975, and that was only as part of Zambia's effort to isolate Rhodesia after Ian Smith's 1965 illegal 'Unilateral Declaration of Independence' (UDI). But all that lay far in the future and there is no doubt that by 1895 Cecil Rhodes had clearly placed his personal imprint on the map of Africa. At the age of barely forty-two he was at the height of his political and financial powers.

Groote Schuur

Rhodes never settled in either of the colonies that bore his name. He visited Rhodesia about once a year, to be lionised by the settlers, but he preferred to make his permanent home closer to the centre of power in Cape Town and in 1891 he leased and later bought an old Cape Dutch house on the eastern side of Table Mountain. Rhodes renamed the house Groote Schuur ('The Great

Groote Schuur, Rhodes's house in Cape Town from 1891, an old Cape Dutch house dating back to the seventeenth century

Granary'), for it had originally been the residence of the Dutch East India Company's senior storekeeper. Though dating back to the seventeenth century, the house had been changed and adapted beyond recognition in the intervening two centuries. Rhodes had a strong sense of history and he hired a young British architect, Herbert Baker, to expand and restore the house to something resembling its original character. The result was a fine example of the Cape Dutch style. The classic lines and grand scale of the house appealed to the imperial character of Rhodes who furnished it in spartan simplicity with rustic hand-made furniture and trophies from the 'Matabele War' of 1893. A huge rear verandah opened onto the eastern slopes of the mountain which Rhodes laid out as open parkland stocked with antelope and ostrich.

After Rhodes's death, from 1910 the house became the official residence of first the Prime Minister and then the executive President of South Africa. Following the ending of white rule and the election of Nelson Mandela as President in 1994, the official residence was moved to the heart of Cape Town, close to the parliament building, and Groote Schuur became a museum.

CHAPTER 7

The Premiership, Gold and the Jameson Raid, 1890-96

Cultivating the Afrikaners

By the early 1880s when Rhodes first entered Parliament, the original Dutch settlers of South Africa, the Boers, were beginning to call themselves Afrikaners. The first Anglo-Boer War of 1880-81 had helped them to develop a new sense of national awareness, and, under the leadership of a wealthy Cape landowner named Jan Hofmeyr, the Afrikaner members of the Cape Legislative Assembly formed a political party called the Afrikaner Bond. Unlike the anti-British republicanism of Paul Kruger's Transvaal, the Afrikaners of the Bond believed in co-operation with the British in matters of defence and trade.

The Debating Chamber of the Cape Legislative Assembly, thought to be in about 1895. Rhodes is seated second from the far end, on the Front Bench on the Speaker's right

There were more Afrikaners than English in the Cape Colony and Rhodes recognised that if British influence was to be maintained and expanded in the region, it would have to be with their cooperation. In his eager acceptance of the Stellalanders' land claims in 1884, Rhodes had hoped to demonstrate that Afrikaners had nothing to fear from British overall control in the region. He followed this up in the late 1880s by paying particular attention in the Cape Assembly to the rural interests of the Afrikaner party. Representing a rural constituency himself, Rhodes always felt he had a special affinity with those who earned their living from the land. And as if to emphasise the point, he frequently referred to his one year's farming experience in Natal as though it were considerably longer. But then Rhodes's recollections of his past were often exaggerated or highly romanticised and it has taken many decades for biographers to disentangle truth from self-inflated myth.

Prime Minister of the Cape, 1890

Throughout the 1880s Rhodes cultivated the friendship of Hofmeyr and the Bond with such success that after the general election of 1890 he commanded the support of a clear majority in the Assembly and thus became Prime Minister.

Rhodes's main contribution to Cape politics during the five and a half years of his premiership evolved out of his determination to solve once and for all what he termed 'the Native Question'. Indeed, in confronting this issue head-on, Rhodes played an important role in defining some of the racial policies that were to form the foundations of the twentieth-century South African state.

Rhodes saw an indelible link between land, labour and political rights. Constitutionally, the Cape Colony had so far been officially nonracist in its attitude to political rights. But the franchise was deliberately restricted by a property qualification which in effect meant that only a tiny minority of black men ever qualified to vote, while virtually every male white colonist was guaranteed a vote. So far, no women, black or white, were eligible to vote anywhere in the empire, not even in Britain itself. But as more African territory was incorporated into the Cape Colony, and with the concurrent spread of mission education, there was a gradual increase in the number of Africans qualifying for the vote. The logical consequence was that Africans would in due course out-vote the white colonists, and then how long would it remain a British colony? Rhodes saw this contradiction more clearly and with less hypocrisy than many of his 'liberal' friends and colleagues.

During his first term in office Rhodes supported legislation that trebled the property qualification for the franchise, added an

A contemporary Punch cartoon (10 December 1892) depicting Rhodes straddling the continent, holding aloft a telegraph line which he hoped would one day stretch 'from Cape to Cairo' From the author's own collection

266   PUNCH, OR THE LONDON CHARIVARI.   [DECEMBER 10, 1892.

THE RHODES COLOSSUS
STRIDING FROM CAPE TOWN TO CAIRO.

income requirement and literacy test and ruled that African land was 'communal' and therefore ineligible for consideration as an individual's property. This deliberately and dramatically cut back African qualification for the vote.

The Glen Grey Act, and the 'Strop Bill'

Rhodes then went on to devise the main piece of legislation that is associated with his name, the Glen Grey Act of 1894. The Act divided the land of Glen Grey district in the Eastern Cape into small individual tenancy plots of ten acres each, just enough to support one couple and a few small children, but not enough to support an extended African family. Furthermore, all fit adult males who failed to engage in wage employment outside the district for at least three months a year were to be charged a 'labour tax'. The latter was intended to 'encourage' black men to work on white-owned farms or in the mines. Finally, as their tiny land holdings were deliberately too small to enable them to qualify for the franchise, the residents of Glen Grey were to be allowed to send elected representatives to an 'advisory council' for their separate local government.

Rhodes considered the Glen Grey Act the flagship of his premiership and recommended that it be extended to the whole of 'British Africa'. In the event it was not extended universally, and the labour tax was dropped, but the Act laid the foundations for the principle of segregated African local government and the deliberate denial of political rights for blacks in 'white' South Africa, which was to become the basis for *apartheid* in the twentieth century.

In the final year of his premiership, Rhodes tried, unsuccessfully, to push through legislation that would legalise the flogging of black and 'coloured' employees in the Cape Colony, for even the most minor of 'offences'. Known as the 'Strop Bill', it was described by the contemporary literary figure and arch critic of Rhodes, Olive Schreiner, as treating employees like slaves.

The Jameson Raid

Through his premiership of the Cape or through the surrogacy of his British South Africa Company, by 1895 Rhodes's writ ran from Cape Town in the south to Lake Tanganyika in the north, a region the size of Western Europe. Through his alliance with the

Afrikaner Bond, he commanded the support of two-thirds of the members of the Cape Parliament. He appeared unassailable, and yet, within a few months he was to resign from the premiership, disgraced and discredited.

It started with disillusionment in Rhodesia. A mining engineer reported very unfavourably on the prospects for gold mining in the territory. The report was suppressed so as not to alarm investors, but its revelations worried Rhodes. With hopes now dashed of a 'second Rand' north of the Limpopo, Rhodes turned his attention to the problems of the gold mining industry in Johannesburg, particularly the high cost of deep-level mining.

Gold mining on the Witwatersrand was mainly in the hands of British mining capitalists, of whom Rhodes was one of the more prominent. But being within the Transvaal republic, their companies were subject to the laws of Kruger's Government. Kruger's main concern was the welfare of his rural Afrikaner subjects, and his government taxed the mining industry heavily, in the interests of the rural Afrikaners. By the mid-1890s there were many thousands of British and other *uitlanders* ('outsiders') living in Johannesburg and Kruger feared that if they had the vote they might soon outnumber his own Afrikaner electorate, overthrow his government and change the republic's laws to suit the interests of the mining industry. He therefore ruled that only white adult males with a minimum of fourteen years' residence were eligible to vote for members of the republic's parliament. An *uitlander* 'Reform Committee' emerged in Johannesburg to protest the injustice of depriving British adults of the vote in a republic in which they paid most of the taxes; but their peaceful agitation produced few tangible results.

Realising the crucial importance of Johannesburg's gold to British strategic interests and distrusting German overtures towards Kruger's Government, quite apart from his own personal financial interests, Rhodes decided that the time had come for bold action. He devised an outrageous plan to stage a *coup* in the Transvaal. It was to start with a 'spontaneous' uprising of *uitlanders* in Johannesburg, which would be supported by a flying-column from his own BSA Company police. The latter had been specially moved down to the border in neighbouring Bechuanaland under the command of the Administrator of Rhodesia, Dr Jameson. Rhodes secretly dispatched truckloads of rifles on the newly opened railway to Johannesburg where his brother Frank and others of the Reform Committee were supposed to organise the rising. But when the time came, the rebellion failed to materialise. Clearly not that many *uitlanders* were concerned enough about the vote to risk their lives in an act of treason.

Undaunted, Jameson decided to go ahead with his side of the operation anyway, claiming he was going to the aid of British 'women and children' in Johannesburg. Jameson had had an inflated notion of his own military capability since his deceptively easy victory over the Amandebele in 1893 and he appears to have thought that news of the approach of his gallant band of men would prompt the *uitlanders* to action. His 'gallant band' crossed the Bechuanaland border on 29 December 1895 only to be surrounded as they approached Johannesburg by the forewarned Transvaalers. After a brief fight in which a number of Jameson's men were killed, they were forced to surrender on 2 January 1896. The leaders of the Johannesburg conspirators had already been arrested and Jameson and his raiders joined them in Pretoria gaol.

The end of political power

Rhodes, from his base in Cape Town, had of course been in overall charge of the scheme from the beginning. This became public knowledge the moment the telegraph wires flashed southwards from Mafeking that Rhodes's trusted lieutenant Jameson had begun his fateful 'Raid' into the Transvaal. The arrest of Frank Rhodes as a conspirator in Johannesburg merely implicated the Cape Prime Minister ever deeper in the plot. A shocked Jan Hofmeyr promptly withdrew the support of the Afrikaner Bond from Rhodes's Government, thus depriving the Prime Minister of a majority in parliament. Even the English members of his Cabinet hurriedly strove to distance themselves from their disgraced former hero, and Rhodes was forced to resign as Prime Minister of the Cape Colony.

Rhodes had used to be a cautious man. Occasionally he had shown signs of a certain recklessness, but steady and sure had been his motto, especially in business matters. From his position

A contemporary drawing showing Rhodes attending the Parliamentary Committee of Inquiry called to investigate the Jameson Raid, Westminster, February 1897. In the Chair is Conservative MP W.L. Jackson. On his right, with an orchid in his lapel, is the Conservative Colonial Secretary Joseph Chamberlain. Rhodes is seated at the witness table in the centre of the room, bluffing his way through the most awkward questions and never once revealing Chamberlain's complicity

of supreme power, however, he seems to have succumbed to the flattery of sycophants and the isolation and corruption of power. Former friends noted a new intolerance and arrogance creeping into his manner and a ruthlessness that at best was amoral. He believed he was invincible, and it took the Jameson Raid to prove him wrong.

In a gesture of reconciliation Kruger magnanimously spared the lives of the leading conspirators. Most were let off with a heavy fine, paid by Rhodes, while Jameson served less than twelve months in prison, most of it in England. The jingoistic British press made much of Jameson's 'heroic dash', and the poet Kipling is reputed to have drawn the inspiration for his famous poem, 'If –', from the plight of Jameson: 'If you can keep your head while all about you are losing theirs and blaming it on you, ...' But the embarrassed British Government could not afford to openly condone such a view and Rhodes was summoned to London.

In fact, the British Colonial Secretary, Joseph Chamberlain, had known all about the Transvaal plot and had secretly approved of Rhodes's plan. Now, after the failure of the Raid, and with a public inquiry in the offing, Chamberlain wanted Rhodes's assurance that his involvement would remain a secret. Rhodes obliged and a grateful British Government ensured that the BSA Company did not lose its Royal Charter.

CHAPTER 8

Crisis in Rhodesia

The Amandebele and Mashona rebellions

Rhodes spent less than a week in London conversing with Joseph Chamberlain in February 1896. A parliamentary inquiry into the Jameson Raid would come the following February. Anxious to avoid public humiliation in Cape Town, he set sail for Rhodesia, via Suez and Mozambique. A few days after his landing in Mozambique, at the end of March 1896, Rhodes received news that the Amandebele had risen in rebellion in western Rhodesia.

For the next few weeks, the Amandebele ranged freely over their former Kingdom (Matabeleland) while those colonists not killed in the initial uprising sought refuge in the heavily defended town of Bulawayo. The Amandebele had never really been defeated in open battle in 1893, nor had they surrendered their arms, but they had been treated very badly by the colonists in the aftermath of conquest. Now that the 'invincible' Jameson was in Pretoria gaol and most of the BSA Company police were out of the country for the Raid, the Amandebele had seized the opportunity to regain their freedom.

Inspired and co-ordinated by spirit mediums of the old religion, they laid siege to Bulawayo, surrounding it on three sides. They left open the western side of the town to enable the colonists to escape to Bechuanaland for the Amandebele had no desire to perpetrate a massacre and provoke an act of British vengeance. In the event, however, this was a fatal error from the Amandebele point of view for it left the way open for British reinforcements from the Cape. Thus, Bulawayo was relieved in June 1896. The Amandebele, however, had learned from their earlier defeat by the British and used guerrilla tactics to continue the fight, rather than trying to take on the highly mobile British forces in open battle. Unable to defeat them, Rhodes authorised the use of scorched-earth tactics to try and starve the 'rebels' into submission. The Amandebele finally retreated into the Matopo Hills to the south of Bulawayo.

Rhodes had been observing events from the Rhodesian capital

of Salisbury in the heart of Mashonaland. Following the relief of Bulawayo, he moved down from Salisbury and took over the direction of the scorched-earth tactics in Matabeleland. No sooner had he done so than the Mashona rose in rebellion in Mashonaland.

Rhodes was now in the most critical position of his career. He had just been forced to resign from the Board of the BSA Company for involving the Company's police in the Transvaal Raid. With rebellion in Rhodesia spreading, the Company's share prices were in danger of collapse. And to cap it all, Rhodes was being summoned back to London to give evidence at an official enquiry into the Jameson Raid, for which, from the British Government's point of view, he was intended to be the scapegoat. His whole personal and political credibility, indeed his whole financial empire, appeared to be hanging in the balance. Somehow, he had to win back the public's confidence and adulation and the only way to do this was to emerge a hero out of the fiasco of the rebellion in Rhodesia.

Indaba with the Amandebele chiefs

There was no quick and easy way to dislodge the Amandebele from the granite fastness of the Matopo Hills. Against the wishes of many of the colonial settlers, who were thirsting for revenge, Rhodes decided it was time for talking, or *indaba*, to use the Isindebele term. But it was essential from Rhodes's point of view, that he should get the credit for the peace. The Amandebele leaders held him responsible for all their recent woes, especially the theft of their cattle and best land, but they allowed him to come unarmed into their stronghold, as they wished to hold him to account. The first of several meetings took place on 21 August 1896. Besides two servants, Rhodes was accompanied by two trusted interpreters: Johann Colenbrander, one of the early 'pioneers', and Johnny Grootboom, an African Christian from the Eastern Cape. He also took his long-term Kimberley friend Dr Hans Saur, and, perhaps most important of all, Vere Stent, the correspondent of *The Cape Times*. If they survived, it was essential that 'Rhodes's *Indaba*' be recorded for posterity, and so it was. The drawing that was widely published to illustrate the colonial view of the *indaba*, shows Rhodes sitting on an anthill, with the Amandebele leaders sitting submissively on the ground in front of him.

Rhodes's Indaba. A contemporary artist's impression. Rhodes is seen here seated on an anthill, with the correspondent from the Cape Times, Vere Stent, taking notes behind him. Seated on Rhodes's right is his interpreter Johann Colenbrander. It is recorded that the original sketch was made by Baden-Powell from information supplied by Stent

There is no doubt that Rhodes displayed immense courage in venturing unarmed into the rebel stronghold: he had earlier declared that he was 'more afraid of being thought afraid'. But the reality of the *indaba* was very different from that portrayed in the colonial illustration.

The Amandebele chiefs and war leaders were incensed, and they let Rhodes know their grievances in no uncertain terms. Rhodes was forced to listen silently while their grievances were translated. What he heard was a bitter indictment of the colonial system, as created by himself and implemented by his 'pioneer' settlers. He held another meeting with the rebels a week later during which one particularly angry young Amandebele soldier threatened him with a gun. When Rhodes rebuked him for coming armed to the *indaba,* the young man replied: 'I find if I talk with my rifle in my hand the white man pays more attention to what I

A group of Amandebele surrendering their rifles, October/November 1896 Photo, Zimbabwe National Archives

say.' Rhodes promised to redress their main grievances and strove to convince them that he really wanted peace. Many informal meetings followed as Rhodes gradually won the confidence of the chiefs, with a third *indaba* on 9 September and the formal submission and the laying down of arms on 13 October.

Although the war in Mashonaland was far from over, the colonial media ensured that Rhodes got full credit for the peace in the west. Financial confidence in the BSA Company was restored; Rhodes returned to England a hero and bluffed his way through the parliamentary enquiry with all his old customary bluster.

Rebellion in Mashonaland

Rebellion in Mashonaland had begun in an uncoordinated fashion, with local outbreaks encouraged by the initial successes of the Amandebele. The apparent ease with which the colonists had been able to seize the land in 1890 had encouraged their belief that the Mashona were a submissive people from whom they had nothing to fear. Thus, when rebellion did occur, it was put down with a savagery worse than anything inflicted on the Amandebele.

Perhaps because of this, contemporaries and subsequent biographers of Rhodes have tended to play it down, preferring to play up the significance of the Amandebele rebellion with its concluding drama of the 'Rhodes's *Indaba*', as though that were the end of resistance to colonial rule in Rhodesia. In fact, rebellion in Mashonaland extended well into the second half of 1897, far longer than the fight in Matabeleland.

Following his performance at the Parliamentary Inquiry in London in February 1897, Rhodes returned to what he regarded as *his* Rhodesia. The Mashona rebellion was to last for many more months and Rhodes was directly involved in authorising the extra-judicial killing of many Mashona 'rebels'. Villages were destroyed by Maxim machine-gun; suspected 'rebels' were hanged from trees; and caves where women and children were sheltering were cleared by dynamite. It was only with methods such as these, that resistance in Mashonaland was finally overcome.

CHAPTER 9

The Final Years: War and Death

The deterioration of British-Boer relations

The fiasco of the Jameson Raid had not only ruined Rhodes's political career; it was also instrumental in pushing South Africa closer towards full-scale war. All Rhodes's careful nurturing of Afrikaner trust was ruined overnight. The Raid helped raise Kruger's anti-British republicanism to new levels of respectability. Kruger could now call on the full support of the Orange Free State and even the sympathy of Afrikaners in the Cape Colony. Furthermore, the German Emperor, on hearing of Jameson's capture, sent a congratulatory telegram to Kruger in which he pledged that Germany would never allow the Transvaal to succumb to outside attack.

The European rivalry which was to lead the world to war in 1914 was already becoming evident by the late 1890s and Britain saw the German telegram as a direct challenge to her own vital strategic interests in southern Africa. Gold underpinned the world's international trading currencies, and Britain was still the world's greatest trading nation. The Witwatersrand, in the heart of Kruger's republic, was the world's largest single source of gold and Britain had hitherto regarded the Transvaal as falling within her own sphere of influence. Clearly the time had come when the Transvaal's goldfields could no longer be allowed to remain within a hostile independent state. Thus, where Rhodes's private enterprise had failed, the British Imperial Government took over.

In 1897 the British Government appointed a staunch imperialist, Lord Alfred Milner, to be British High Commissioner to South Africa. Milner immediately began to build up British troops in the Cape Colony and Natal, and during 1898 and 1899 he kept up a continual barrage of demands for reform within the Transvaal, including the granting of full voting rights to the *uitlanders*, a demand which, if complied with, would effectively have brought about an end to Kruger's independent government. Kruger could see what was coming and under pressure from his young and over-confident generals he issued an ultimatum demanding the immediate withdrawal of British troops from his borders. When the ultimatum expired on 12 October 1899, Afrikaner forces from the Orange Free State and the Transvaal crossed the border into the Cape and Natal. The South African War (or the Boer War as it is often known) had begun.

The war begins

In throwing his tiny army against the might of the British Empire, Kruger hoped for some quick early victories that would prompt a British backdown, as had happened in the Transvaal in 1881. Despite some early successes, however, the initial impetus was soon lost, and the Afrikaner armies became involved in laying siege to Mafeking and Kimberley in the northern Cape Colony, and Ladysmith in Natal. Meanwhile the British had time to assemble a massive army from all quarters of the Empire.

Once it had become obvious that war was inevitable, Rhodes was determined to be somewhere in the thick of it. As he was now excluded from the corridors of power in Cape Town, he decided to make for the one place where his word was still virtually law, the diamond city of Kimberley. He caught the last train north from Cape Town and arrived in Kimberley just a few hours before the invading Afrikaner army cut the town off from the outside world.

The siege of Kimberley

Rhodes was a difficult man to share a siege with. Frustrated at not being able to direct the war itself, he interfered in the defence of Kimberley and refused to bow to the orders of the commanding officer, Colonel Kekewich. Almost the whole of Kimberley belonged to De Beers and Rhodes ensured that his company continued to play its usual dominant role in the life of the town. He ordered the closing of the diamond mines for the duration of the siege, because of lack of coal, and to conserve food supplies, most of the African mine labourers were expelled from the city. When food rations ran low, Rhodes organised the Company's resources to dole out 'siege soup' to those of the white population who were in need. He then ordered that the mining shafts be opened to provide the white women and children of Kimberley with shelter from the daily shelling of the enemy's artillery. In response to the latter, the company's engineers cast a huge cannon which, to the obvious delight of Rhodes, they nick-named 'Long Cecil'. To the surprise of all, the cannon proved very effective, firing homemade shells anything up to five miles. It was claimed that engraved on the body of some of the shells was the inscription, 'with the compliments of C.J. Rhodes'!

The soup kitchen at the siege of Kimberley. Rhodes, in dark jacket and white flannels is perched against the wall with hat in hand, and the African servants who will prepare the soup, sitting in subservient position in the foreground

Other activities of Rhodes were not so universally welcomed. In direct contravention of Colonel Kekewich's orders, Rhodes used African employees of De Beers to run the blockade and thus provide himself with an unofficial and private communication service with the outside world. In these messages, to Cape politicians and British military officers, he constantly undermined the authority of Kekewich. Rhodes sought to create the impression that he alone was keeping the town together and keeping morale high. He could not understand why the advancing British column was not making greater effort to raise the siege of Kimberley and liberate Cecil Rhodes. In messages to military officers, he grossly exaggerated the imminent danger to the town. There is little doubt that because of Rhodes's urgent demands for help, which he deliberately leaked to the press, the new British commander in South Africa, Field-Marshal Lord Roberts, gave greater priority to the relief of Kimberley than the military situation would otherwise have warranted.

In fact the presence of Rhodes in Kimberley had acted to assist the relatively weak British position in the early months of the war, for the invading Afrikaner army made it a priority to capture Cecil Rhodes. They thus maintained a strong military presence around the town at a time when, strategically, they would have been better served pushing south into the undefended Cape Colony and arousing the Cape Afrikaners in their support.

After four frustrating months of siege Kimberley was finally relieved on 15 February 1900. By the end of June, Ladysmith and Mafeking had been relieved and all the principal towns and railways of the Afrikaner republics were in British hands. It looked to many, including Rhodes, as if the war was over. The Afrikaner generals, however, did not come forward to surrender. They took to the bush and conducted a further two years of determined guerrilla warfare. But the British use of armoured trains, barbed-wire, blockhouses, burning of farms and confinement of Afrikaner women and children and their African servants to segregated concentration camps finally ground down their resistance and forced them into submission in May 1902. By then Rhodes was already in his grave.

The death of Rhodes

Rhodes had had premonitions of an early death ever since his two heart-attacks in Kimberley during the 1870s and it is generally assumed that this foreboding helps account for the acute sense of urgency with which he pushed forward his ideas. The strains of 1896 must have taken their toll and during 1900 and 1901 his heart weakened, and his health steadily declined. The doctors could do little more than ease the pain and relieve his breathing.

He took a small cottage by the sea, at Muizenberg on the east side of the Cape Peninsular. And there, with Jameson and a few other close friends at his bedside, Cecil Rhodes died at 6 p.m. on 26 March 1902. His banker and principal early biographer, Sir Lewis Michell, who was at his deathbed, recorded his final words as, 'So little done, so much to do'.

CHAPTER 10

Conclusion

There are signs that in the early months of the South African War Rhodes had every intention of resurrecting his shattered political career. Certainly, he presumed he would be involved in the post-war reconstruction of South Africa, and indeed, he almost certainly would have been, had his life not been cut so short. Rhodes had a very clear vision of a great new Anglo-Afrikaner federation, under the protection of the British flag, which would stretch from Cape Town to the Zambezi and so include his beloved colony of Rhodesia.

Rhodes and 'equal rights'

Shortly after the raising of the siege of Kimberley, Rhodes expounded his ideas to a meeting of the shareholders of De Beers. He declared that his guiding principle for the new British dominion of South Africa would be 'equal rights for every white man south of the Zambezi'. It was a deliberate attempt to revive his Afrikaner alliance of former years, to show that the British would be magnanimous in victory and that even a defeated Afrikaner nation could expect equality and justice within the new South Africa. But Rhodes's olive branch attracted little favourable acclaim. On the contrary, it caused considerable embarrassment to those of his liberal parliamentary colleagues who owed their seats to those black and mixed-race voters from the Cape who had managed to surmount the stringent franchise qualifications which Rhodes himself had helped restrict still further.

Under pressure from these, Rhodes had to change his 'guiding principle' to 'equal rights for every *civilized* man south of the Zambezi'. And so was born a famous slogan that Rhodes's admirers were later to claim proved their hero's underlying non-racial stance. But to follow that interpretation is to blind oneself to the truth. Rhodes, like most of his contemporary Britons, was an avowed imperialist. But where some of his more liberal-minded colleagues clung to the notion that the British Empire was a benevolent project, Rhodes understood more clearly than most that imperialism was fundamentally a racist project, and he pursued it ruthlessly. Thus, the original version of his 'guiding principle' expressed his true feelings on the question of civil rights in southern Africa.

His Glen Grey Act of 1894 had set out the foundations for South Africa's twentieth-century racial segregation which was to evolve into the system of *apartheid* that ruled South Africa from 1948 to 1994. And, quite apart from his conquests and violent suppression of rebellion, on the domestic front, his attempt to pass the 'Strop Bill' in 1895 showed the extent to which he was prepared to violate the human rights of black and 'coloured' people in southern Africa. Rhodes would have approved the Act of Union of 1909, which combined the two British colonies and two former Afrikaner/Boer republics into one South African state. He would also have approved the constitution of the Union, which left the future destiny of South Africa firmly in the hands of white South Africans.

The Rhodes Scholarships

Ever a practical man, prepared to compromise when faced with hard reality, Rhodes ultimately was driven in his declining years to adapt his 'great idea'. The final version of his Will left his estate to a Trust fund under the supervision of Lord Rothschild. But instead of being used to form a secret society dedicated to the furtherance of the British Empire, the fund was now to provide scholarships for the younger sons of the 'white' dominions, and the United States, to study at Oxford and so promote 'the union of the English-speaking people throughout the world'. In a final codicil, it included some German scholars, to improve co-operation between the English and the Germans. Over the years 'Rhodes Scholars' have risen to positions of prominence in their respective countries. It has been adapted over the years and now includes black and brown scholars as well as white, and competition for the annual scholarships has become extremely fierce. There is even a Mandela-Rhodes Foundation which draws funds from the Rhodes Trust. The concept of the Rhodes Scholarships has thus proven far more enduring than the Empire they were originally conceived to promote.

The Rhodes legacy

In his day Rhodes personified the late Victorian drive for empire. His example and audacity attracted those younger sons of middle-class England who, like himself, sought glory, fame and fortune overseas. Their deeds provided inspiration for some of the leading literary populists of the day, such as Henry Rider-Haggard, Rudyard Kipling and John Buchan. Rhodes certainly achieved much in his forty-nine years and the clear-sighted ruthlessness with which he wielded power has fascinated biographer after biographer over the decades since his death. Unfortunately, the fascination has often been so great that it has sometimes been difficult to discern where reality ends and myth begins. There can be no doubt that Rhodes's segregationist policies went some way towards laying the foundations for South Africa's *apartheid* state. The violence he directed towards black people, especially in 'Rhodesia' were a fundamental part of Rhodes's legacy. And the degree to which a particular brand of overt racism persisted among many 'Rhodesians' throughout the colonial period and led to the defiant Rhodesian UDI of 1965–1979 was one of the more unsavoury legacies of Rhodes's own championing of white supremacist ideals.

Although Rhodes's name is now removed from modern maps of Africa, and replaced by Zambia and Zimbabwe, Rhodes's ghost lives on.

FURTHER READING

Biographies of Rhodes

A selection of some of the principal biographies of Rhodes, in chronological order of publication:

Imperialist (pseudonym for Revd. John Verschoyle), *Cecil Rhodes: A Biography and an Appreciation* (1897).

Vindex (pseudonym for Revd. John Verschoyle), *Cecil Rhodes: His Political Life and Speeches, 1881-1900* (1900).

Lewis Michell, *The Life of the Rt. Hon. Cecil John Rhodes, 1853-1902*, 2 Volumes (1910). The first full-length biography.

James G. McDonald, *Rhodes: A Life* (1927). Based mostly on personal recollection and conversations with Rhodes.

Basil Williams, *Cecil Rhodes* (1938).

Felix Gross, *Rhodes of Africa* (1956).

J.G. Lockhart and C.M. Woodhouse, *Cecil Rhodes: The Colossus of Southern Africa* (1963).

John Flint, *Cecil Rhodes* (1974). The first seriously critical biography which contains the complete text of the 'Confession of Faith'.

Apollon B. Davidson, *Cecil Rhodes and His Time* (translated from the original Russian, 1988). Particularly interesting for its Russian perspective and the focus on the British culture of Rhodes's time.

Robert I. Rotberg, *The Founder: Cecil Rhodes and the Pursuit of Power* (1988). The most comprehensive biography to date.

Anthony Thomas, *Rhodes* (1996). The book that accompanied a BBC television series.

Titles related to the life of Rhodes

The best introduction to Kimberley for the general reader is: Brian Roberts, *Kimberley: Turbulent City* (1976). See also, the same author's *The Diamond Magnates* (1972).

More specialised analyses of the city and its diamond business, including the role of Rhodes, are to be found in:

Rob Turrell, *Capital and Labour on the Kimberley Diamond Fields* (1987);

William Worger, *South Africa's City of Diamonds* (1987); and Colin Newbury, *The Diamond Ring* (1989).

For the impact of the diamond fields on the hinterland of Kimberley and for Rhodes's role in the acquisition of southern Bechuanaland, see:

Kevin Shillington, *The Colonisation of the Southern Tswana* (1985); while for Rhodes's attempt to annex the Bechuanaland Protectorate (modern Botswana), see: Neil Parsons, *King Khama, Emperor Joe and the Great White Queen* (1998).

For the activities of Rhodes and other mining capitalists in the early years of the Witwatersrand goldfields, see:

Geoffrey Wheatcroft, *The Randlords* (1986).

The best account of the founding and early years of the British South Africa Company remains:

John S. Galbraith, *Crown and Charter* (1974); while for the classic African viewpoint on the founding of Rhodesia, see:

Stanlake Samkange, *Origins of Rhodesia* (1968).

Although some of his interpretations have been questioned by academics, Terrence Ranger's *Revolt in Southern Rhodesia, 1896–97* (2nd edition 1979) remains the standard detailed work on the Amandebele and Mashona rebellions.

For an authoritative account of the Jameson Raid see:

Elizabeth Longford, *Jameson's Raid* (2nd edition, 1982).

For the South African War of 1899–1902, the most comprehensive narrative account remains: Thomas Pakenham, *The Boer War* (1979); while for a highly readable account of the zone of conflict of specific concern to Cecil Rhodes, see: Brian Gardner, *The Lion's Cage: The Siege of Kimberley* (1969).

For the Rhodes Trust and Scholarships see: Philip Ziegler, *Legacy. Cecil Rhodes, the Rhodes Trust and the Rhodes Scholarships* (2008).

For the controversy over the Rhodes' statues, see:

Rhodes Must Fall Movement, Oxford, *Rhodes Must Fall. The Struggle to Decolonise the Racist Heart of Empire*, edited by Roseanne Chantiluke, Brian Kwoba and Athinangamso Nkopo (2018).